# HAMPTON COURT PALACE

*Above: Bird's eye view of the Palace*
*Over page:    East Front and gardens in winter.*
*At right: Carved heads adorn the keystones of the cloistral arches in Fountain Court.*

# CONTENTS

*In 1769 Wolsey's Great Gatehouse was found to be in danger of collapse. The top two floors were removed and the remainder extensively rebuilt.*

# INTRODUCTION

R ICH OR POOR, high born or humble, the English like to make their homes their own. Hence the saying 'an Englishman's home is his castle.' When they move into a new house, they change it to suit their own tastes and way of life. It is the same story with any English house, large or small, centuries or merely decades old.

And so it has been with Hampton Court Palace. The Kings and Queens of England from Henry VIII to the present day have all left their mark. Almost every monarch has made changes to the Palace and its gardens. Some monarchs lavished large amounts of money on its fabric and furnishings and made frequent visits. Others were more neglectful and also allowed furnishings and other contents to be removed for use in the other royal palaces.

*Anne Boleyn's Gateway was built by Wolsey but has been much altered since. The small bell tower on top dates from the eighteenth century. The clock was brought here by William IV and the doorway and windows were restored in Queen Victoria's reign.*

*The height of the storeys reflects the importance of the rooms: arches for the low ground floor, long windows and circular lights for the State Apartments and small square windows for the courtier lodgings in the top storey.*

*The north-east corner of Wren's classical court abuts the rich red brickwork of the Tudor Palace.*

*Crimson velvet bed sold to William III by Lord Jersey, his Lord Chamberlain. Royal Collection, Hampton Court Palace.*

What the visitor sees today is a harmonious blend of Tudor and English Baroque architecture. Hampton Court viewed from the West Gate is Henry VIII's Tudor Palace, while Sir Christopher Wren's Baroque facade overlooks the formal gardens and Long Water to the east. Inside the State and Private Apartments the visitor can see part of where the Tudor court lived. Wren's beautiful Fountain Court and most of the sumptuous State Apartments are on view, as well as the smaller and more intimate Private Apartments. Pictures, furniture and tapestries from the Royal Collection decorate many of the rooms.

To visit Hampton Court Palace and its gardens is to experience nearly five centuries of English history. Thanks to the continuing programme of restoration, dating back to the reign of Queen Victoria, the Palace has endured to become one of England's most popular tourist attractions.

*Margaret Cecil, Countess of Ranelagh, one of Sir Godfrey Kneller's Hampton Court Beauties. Royal Collection, Hampton Court Palace.*

Clock Court. Originally known as Fountain Court because of a trick waterwork which stood here. Elizabethan visitors noted that "you can, if you like, make the water play upon the ladies and others who are standing by, and give them a thorough wetting".

## HISTORY

Hampton Court has been a royal palace since Cardinal Wolsey presented it to Henry VIII in 1525, as a gift, and has been used by the monarchy throughout its long history. Although it has been open to the public since 1838, the Palace remains the property of Her Majesty The Queen, and is still used by the royal family for state occasions and charity functions, as well as privately. The Department of the Environment has overall responsibility for its administration, care and maintenance.

## TUDORS

HAMPTON COURT PALACE was begun in 1514 by Thomas Wolsey early in Henry VIII's reign on the site of a house leased from the Knights Hospitallers. Wolsey was exceptionally able, active, worldly and rich. Already Archbishop of York, he became a cardinal and Lord Chancellor in 1515. The young King relied heavily on his skill in state affairs. His London house as Archbishop was York Place, Westminster. But he resolved to replace the Hospitallers' manor house by the Thames at Hampton Court with a new country residence grand enough to reflect his dignity and ambition.

Thomas Wolsey, painted around 1520, in his cardinal's scarlet biretta and robes. Artist Unknown.

The Poet Skelton wrote:
"More like a god celestial,
than any creature mortal,
With wordly pomp incredible".

Wolsey Entertains by Joseph Nash. The Cardinal reportedly had 280 silk beds in readiness for visitors.

South-east corner of the Tudor Palace, drawn around 1660 but probably little changed since the days of Henry VIII. Behind the royal apartments looms the top of the Great Hall, the only building shown here which still survives.

*The mass of chimneys — some original, some careful restorations — reflects the greater wealth and comfort of the Tudor era.*

Leading physicians pronounced the site healthy but Wolsey, careful of such matters, ordered the installation of an elaborate drainage system emptying into the river. Three miles of lead pipe brought spring water from Coombe Hill. Stone was supplied from Caen and Reigate, timber from Weybridge and Reading. The distinctive red and purple bricks were baked nearby. Wolsey acquired the richest carpets, tapestries, furniture and fittings, and commissioned the finest artists and craftsmen to decorate his new palace.

*Portraits of Henry VIII have become the most familiar image of a British monarch. Painted after Holbein, King Henry is shown here in his mid forties, when over-indulgence, failed marriages and illness were beginning to take their toll.*

*Part of the Field of Cloth of Gold, artist unknown. Royal Collection, Hampton Court Palace. Henry VIII, Wolsey and their huge procession enter Guisnes in June 1520 to confer with Francis I of France. The guns of the castle fire in salute, startling the swans on the moat. The dragon overhead may represent a firework in the form of a salamander released on 25 June as part of the celebrations.*

The new house contained outer and inner courts, a hall, chapel and kitchens. Splendid apartments were provided for Wolsey, and for Henry and his first queen, Catherine of Aragon, on their visits. The palace also included lodgings for Wolsey's large household and numerous guests. Business took up much of Wolsey's time, even at Hampton Court, involving lavish entertainment for ambassadors and diplomats. With building almost completed by 1525, Wolsey, perhaps fearing the King's envy, judiciously presented him with Hampton Court in return for Richmond Palace.

The poet Skelton's satire had hit home:
*Why come ye not to Court?*
*To which court?*
*To the king's court*
*Or to Hampton Court?*
*Nay, to the king's court.*
*The king's court*
*Should have the excellence*
*But Hampton Court*
*Hath the pre-eminence.*

*North Cloister was the main route by which food and drink were carried from the kitchens and cellars to the Great Hall and other apartments above.*

*In 1521 Wolsey paid £20 for eight roundels of Roman emperors by Maiano. That of Augustus on Anne Boleyn's Gate retains some of its original gilding and colour.*

*The Wolsey Rooms date from the reign of Henry VIII and may once have been used by Wolsey himself, his officials or his guests.*

*Four elephants pull the triumphal car of Fame, from the Flemish tapestry "The Triumph of Fame over Death". Part of the Royal Collection, it was acquired by Wolsey from the Bishopric of Durham in 1523 and now hangs in the Great Watching Chamber.*

*Wyngaerde's drawing shows Hampton Court from the river in 1558. The Great Gatehouse on the left survives in a reduced form and the Great Hall in the centre also still stands, though without the grand towering opening in the roof which allowed smoke to escape from the open fire. Most of the other buildings, including the royal apartments and the river-side gallery, have gone.*

Following Wolsey's failure to secure Henry's divorce, he was stripped of his lands and possessions, and died in 1530 just before he was to be tried for treason. York Palace became the nucleus of the King's new Palace of Whitehall. At Hampton Court Henry replaced Wolsey's Great Hall with a grander one, begun in 1532. The Chapel Royal was remodelled and new kitchens added. He built Cloister Green Court on the site of the present Fountain Court, incorporating fine new royal lodgings, galleries, chambers, a library and baths. New wine and beer cellars supplied the daily drink ration for the thousand or more members of the royal household who accompanied the King when he was in residence. Elaborate gardens were laid out. Tennis courts, bowling alleys and a tiltyard, in addition to the parks stocked with deer and game, catered for Henry's love of sport.

*John Vardy's perspective view of the Great Hall was dedicated to George II.*

*Henry VIII's royal arms appear on the two outer gatehouses.*

In 1536 Henry was betrothed to Jane Seymour at Hampton Court after his second queen, Anne Boleyn, had been beheaded for misconduct. A year later Jane died at the Palace after giving birth to the future Edward VI. The christening held in the Chapel was a splendid occasion. During the late 1540s Henry enjoyed more domesticated years at Hampton Court with his sixth and last queen, Catherine Parr.

*Edward VI was christened at Hampton Court on 15 October 1537. He was carried to Chapel by Lady Exeter under a rich canopy. The procession included the Princesses Mary and Elizabeth and Archbishop Cranmer.*

*Edward VI, attributed to Guillim Stretes. Royal Collection, Hampton Court Palace. Painted around 1550, it shows the thirteen year old King imitating his father's imperious stance.*

*East Front of Hampton Court in the mid-seventeenth century. The Stuart Royal Tennis Court can be seen on the far right. In the centre is the Queen's Long Gallery, built in the 1530s to link the Queen's apartments with the royal nursery on the north side of the Palace.*

*Anne Boleyn, artist unknown. Henry VIII's second wife did not impress the Venetian Ambassador: "not one of the handsomest women in the world, she is of middling stature, swarthy complexion, long neck, wide mouth, bosom not much raised".*

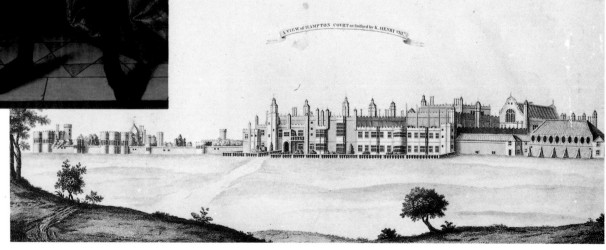

Elizabeth I, artist unknown.
Royal Collection, Hampton Court Palace.
A visiting ambassador noted that: 'In one chamber were several excessively rich tapestries, which are hung up when the queen gives audience to foreign ambassadors: there are numbers of cushions ornamented with gold and silver; many counterpanes and coverlids of beds lined in ermine, in short, all the walls of the palace shine with gold and silver. Here is besides a certain cabinet called Paradise, where besides that everything glitters so with silver, gold and jewels, as to dazzle one's eyes, there is a musical instrument made all of glass, except for the strings.'

The long reign, from 1558 to 1603, of Elizabeth I, Henry's younger daughter, succeeded the brief ones of her half-brother Edward and half-sister Mary, who at one stage held Elizabeth prisoner in the Water Gallery. Early in her reign the Queen nearly died of smallpox at Hampton Court. Perhaps for that reason she seems to have much preferred her palaces at Richmond and Nonsuch, the fanciful creations of her grandfather, Henry VII, and father respectively. Though she did not lavish money on new works, a new privy kitchen was built at Hampton Court in 1567. The jewel of Elizabeth's palace was the sumptuous Paradise Chamber, in Cloister Green Court, with its Persian tapestries, bedecked throne and painted ceiling. The 'well dressed public' was allowed to pay to admire it when the Queen was not in residence. It was later replaced by Wren.

*View of Hampton Court Palace, circa 1640, artist unknown.*
*Royal Collection, Hampton Court Palace.*
*The state barge is rowed by oarsmen in scarlet livery and carries the royal arms on the stern. The three seated figures may be Charles I and two of his sons. This picture provides the clearest surviving view of the river frontage of the late Tudor and early Stuart palace.*

*James I, by Paul van Somer. Royal Collection, Windsor Castle. The Banqueting House in Whitehall can be seen through the window.*

## STUARTS

JAMES I spent his first Christmas at Hampton Court in 1603. His Company of Comedians performed before him and his queen, Anne of Denmark, in the Great Hall. Shakespeare may have acted here in Christmas 1604, in his own *Measure for Measure*. Early that year James presided over the Hampton Court Conference in a vain attempt to settle church differences. It did, however, result in the compilation of the King James or Authorised Version of The Bible. Charles I, the next Stuart ruler, enriched the palace with part of his splendid art collection. This included Andrea Mantegna's *Triumph of Caesar*. Local people were outraged when he created the 11 mile Longford River to feed Hampton Court's ponds and ornamental waters.

*Charles I, by Anthony Van Dyck. Royal Collection, Windsor Castle. Part of a triple view of the King sent to Bernini in Rome, from which he could create a likeness. The completed bust was returned to England as a gift from the Pope to the Catholic Queen.*

*Charles II and his bride Catherine of Braganza, arrived at Hampton Court on 30 May 1662. John Evelyn, who witnessed the event, thought Catherine "of low stature, prettily shaped, languishing and excellent eyes, her teeth wronging her mouth by sticking out little too far; for the rest, lovely enough".*

*Samuel Cooper's miniature
of Oliver Cromwell. Some items at Hampton Court
were saved for Cromwell's use,
but most were sold in 1649-51, including
Henry VIII's cane staff and hawking glove,
dog collars, song books and
a pair of broken organs.*

*On visiting the Palace in June 1662,
John Evelyn reported that the Long Water,
Charles II's new eastern "canal", was "now
near perfected".*

It was to Hampton Court that Charles fled from London in 1642 following his unsuccessful attempt to arrest five members of Parliament. Victorious over the King's forces at Naseby in 1645, the Parliamentarians took over Hampton Court, sealing the doors of the state apartments and removing or smashing 'Popish pictures and superstitious images' in the Chapel. By 1647 Charles was back at the Palace as a prisoner. Negotiations between him and Oliver Cromwell failed and he subsequently escaped to the Isle of Wight. He was eventually captured at Newark, imprisoned at Hampton Court, tried and executed in front of the Banqueting House in Whitehall, in 1649.

Parliament inventoried Hampton Court and other royal possessions. Much was sold but Hampton Court Palace and its parks, and Whitehall Palace, were granted to Cromwell, styled Lord Protector in 1653. He spent weekends at Hampton Court, often working but also hunting and enjoying music and ceremonial. Following the restoration of Charles II, major repairs to the now rather dilapidated Palace were set in hand. In 1662 Charles and his new Queen, Catherine of Braganza, spent three months at Hampton Court following their marriage. Home Park, to the east, was formally landscaped, with the creation of the Long Water and the planting of lime avenues. Neither Charles nor his brother James, who briefly succeeded him, paid more than short visits to the Palace, though Charles sometimes played tennis there at six o'clock in the morning.

The second great era of building at Hampton Court began after William of Orange, Stadtholder of the Netherlands and his wife Mary, James's elder daughter, jointly ascended the throne in 1689 at Parliament's invitation. Finding London's fog and smoke worsened his asthma, William chose Hampton Court as his principal out-of-town residence. Its surroundings were said to remind him of Holland. But the Tudor palace was considered old fashioned and Sir Christopher Wren, Surveyor of the King's Works, was therefore commissioned to replace it with a palace to rival the new Versailles of William's great antagonist Louis XIV.

*William III and Mary II, by Willem Wissing. Royal Collection, Windsor Castle. In 1685 James II sent Wissing to Holland to paint the royal couple. Walpole noted how Wissing ensured that his females would have a healthy glow: "When any lady came to sit to him whose complexion was any ways pale, he would commonly take her by the hand and dance her about the room till she became warmer".*

*Sir Christopher Wren,*
*by Johann Baptist Closterman.*
*Painted in the mid 1690s when the architect was*
*completing St Paul's as well as undertaking*
*work at Greenwich and Hampton Court. At this*
*time, Wren had use of a small office on the west*
*side of Fountain Court. He died at his house on*
*Hampton Court Green in 1723.*

One of Wren's early designs included a grand new entrance, crowned by a central dome. Henry's Great Hall alone was to remain, as focus of a grand avenue through Bushy Park to the north. A more modest project was eventually adopted, largely because of William's haste and wish to obtain the best effect possible at reasonable cost. Only Cloister Green Court was pulled down to be replaced by the present Fountain Court containing new state apartments for the King and Queen, and lodgings for the court. By screening the rest of the Tudor buildings Wren created the illusion of a completely new palace. Although very involved with his new Cathedral of St Paul's and other work, Wren spent much time at Hampton Court, where the shell of the new building was largely complete by mid 1693.

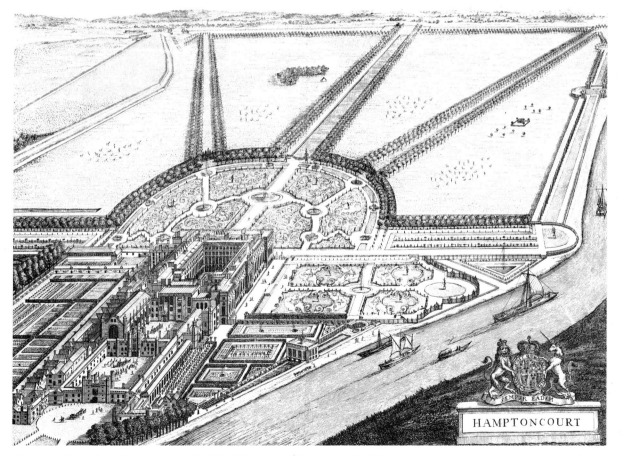

*Hampton Court from the south-west, by John Kip, circa 1705.*
*William III and Mary II had the gardens around the Palace*
*replanned and experimented with foreign and exotic plants, some*
*brought on in hot-houses heated by stoves. Among the plants*
*grown at the Palace at this time were cinnamon, blackwood cedar*
*and wild peas and olives from Barbados, Providence cotton,*
*"red flat painted beans with black streaks" and "Incognita*
*from the East Indies, a bitter taste". One of the gardeners was*
*paid £250 to go to Virginia and collect native specimens.*

The Long Water was shortened to accommodate a parterre on the east front, designed by Daniel Marot, a Huguenot, who had worked for William in Holland. The Tudor Water Gallery, beside the river, was refurbished as temporary apartments for Mary, as William was often away on campaign or in Holland. New gardens were laid out close by as she, like her husband, loved gardening.

When Mary died in 1694 of smallpox, William had work at Hampton Court stopped. Only in 1698, when Whitehall burned down and Europe was briefly at peace, did he order his new apartments to be fitted up. By 1699 the new approach through Bushy Park was complete. In 1700 William ordered that the Water Gallery should be demolished. The present Banqueting House was built further west overlooking the river. While hunting at Hampton Court in 1702, William was thrown from his horse and died soon after at Kensington Palace.

*William III and Mary II's monogram. Their entwined initials beneath a crown — from one of the Delft tulip vases designed to order in the 1690s. Royal Collection, Hampton Court Palace.*

*The King's Second Presence Chamber, by James Stephanoff, from W H Pyne's History of the Royal Residences, 1819. King William occasionally dined here in public, but the room was little used at that time and was often referred to simply as the "next" or "betwixt room".*

*William III and Mary II's love of gardening is reflected both in the Pond Gardens to the south of the Palace (above) and in the Fountain Garden to the east (below), shown here in an engraving made around 1700. A resident mole-catcher was employed full-time at a salary of £16 per year.*

*Bird's Eye View of Hampton Court Palace, early eighteenth century, by Leonard Knyff.*
*Royal Collection, Hampton Court Palace.*
*Viewed from the east around 1708-10, the villages of East Molesey can be seen on the left and Hampton in the distance.*

*Queen Anne, by Sir Godfrey Kneller.*
*Royal Collection, Kensington Palace.*
*In 1704 a short poem by Morden*
*was published in praise of Anne at Hampton Court:*
*"Here our blest Queen's magnificence yet reigns,*
*O'er death's proud empire and its mournful trains.*
*Here Italy and Spain are clearly seen,*
*In richest fruits, trees, shades, in walks and greens".*

His sister-in-law Anne, who succeeded him, preferred Windsor Castle and Kensington Palace but commanded that some of the outstanding work at Hampton Court be completed, and attended council meetings there. Pope's *Rape of the Lock,* based on a real incident after card play at the Palace, includes the famous couplet – tea then being pronounced 'tay':

*Here thou, great Anna, whom three realms obey*
*Dost sometimes counsel take – and sometimes tea.*

The Chapel was refitted in 1711-12 and the Diana Fountain, in the Privy Garden in William's time, was moved to the basin in Bushy Park in 1713. The gardens on the east front were remodelled and the enclosing canal dug.

*Hanoverian royal arms by Grinling Gibbons over the chimney in the Public Dining Room.*

# HANOVERIANS

*The Family of Frederick, Prince of Wales, by George Knapton. Royal Collection, Hampton Court Palace. Painted shortly after the death of Prince Frederick in 1751, the Princess is seen in mourning wearing a black veil. She is sitting in a chair of state beneath a canopy bearing Frederick's arms. A portrait of her late husband hangs in the background, while his eldest son, the future King George III, sits on the left.*

WILLIAM III's Palace enjoyed its heyday during the reigns of George I and II as a favourite summer residence of the Court. Between July and October 1716 while the King was in Hanover, the Prince and Princess of Wales presided over a witty and vivacious court when the Palace was the scene of constant balls, parties, boating trips and other amusements. The years 1716-18 saw the final completion of the Queen's Apartments for the use of the Prince and Princess and the fitting up of the lodgings for their young family.

After the Prince's expulsion from court, George I spent the summer of 1718 at Hampton Court alone. The King's preference was for a secluded existence in his Private Apartments in the company of his two German mistresses. But on this occasion, to counteract the threat that the Prince's court would become a focus of political opposition, he laid on uncharacteristically lavish assemblies and balls. The Royal Tennis Court was fitted up for billiards and cards, plays were again given in the Great Hall and the King dined in public.

*Public Dining Room. Decorated in 1716-18 for the Prince of Wales it was originally intended as a music and dancing room. Its present name dates back to the reign of George II.*

*Hampton Court from the south-east during the reign of George II. Clipped conical yews were very much in fashion.*

In 1732 William Kent remodelled the decayed Tudor state apartments on the east side of Clock Court as lodgings for the young Duke of Cumberland, the future 'Butcher of Culloden'. The walls and ceiling of the Queen's Staircase were decorated in 1734, also by Kent. George II and Queen Caroline spent some summers at Hampton Court between 1728 and 1737 but the gaieties of their visits as Prince and Princess were not repeated.

*During the 1730s the Duke of Cumberland was allocated a presence chamber, bed-chamber, drawing room and four closets in the new east range of Clock Court.*

*George II and Caroline, as Prince and Princess of Wales, and their son Frederick, later Prince of Wales, are portrayed in the coving of the ceiling of the Queen's State Bedchamber. The room was painted in 1715 by James Thornhill, who was both cheaper and considered a better workman than his predecessor, Verrio.*

*The royal arms of Hanover supported by the Trophy Gate lion.*

HAMPTON COURT ceased to be a royal residence under George III. He preferred Windsor Castle and Kew Palace as out-of-town residences. The Great Gatehouse, which had become dangerous, was cut down by two storeys in 1770. Many of the contents of the state rooms went to furnish other palaces. The rest of the palace was divided into apartments granted by royal 'grace-and-favour' to private persons thought deserving. During the late eighteenth century and early nineteenth century fashionable social life continued at Hampton Court but only among these residents.

George IV came to Hampton Court only to view the Royal Stud in Home Park, and had many statues and vases in the gardens removed to Windsor. William IV, King from 1830 to 1837, appointed his queen, Adelaide, Ranger of Bushy Park, a post he had held as Prince. He restored the King's Staircase, and replaced the by now inaccurate Tudor Astronomical Clock in Clock Court with a clock from St James's Palace. The State Apartments were fitted with pictures from other palaces, so paving the way for the young Queen Victoria to open the Apartments free to the public in 1838. Hampton Court soon became a favourite outing for Londoners, especially after the railway opened in 1849.

*Rowlandson's watercolour may record a rare visit by George III or his eldest son to the Palace, but for the most part Hampton Court was at this time the preserve of grace-and-favour residents and a few trippers.*

*By the mid-nineteenth century up to 180,000 people a year were visiting the Palace. On summer Saturdays a military band would play by the East Front to entertain visitors. In 1847 The Times applauded the existence of "places of of healthful amusement" near London which could reverse "the deterioration in the physique of our population".*

*During the late 1840s the Chapel ceiling was repaired, repainted and regilded, though only after a long squabble over the cost and extent of the work.*

*The Chapel Royal, Hampton Court by James D Wingfield, 1849. Regular services continue to be held in the Chapel.*

# VICTORIAN RESTORATION

During the 1840s, the Office of Works began to restore Tudor Hampton Court to its 'original gorgeous and artistic beauty', disfigured, it was now thought, by later alterations and additions. It replaced lost Tudor chimneys and other features and restored the Chapel roof and the Great Hall. In the 1870s, main drainage replaced Wolsey's brick sewers and the Astronomical Clock was reinstated, at the plea of Ernest Law, a grace-and-favour resident who wrote a monumental history of the palace.

The Great Gatehouse was again remodelled and the vault beneath Anne Boleyn's Gateway renewed. Most of this work, of 1882, was done in harsh red brick and Bath Stone. Wolsey's Closet and the Horn Room were opened to the public. In front of the Tudor palace Wolsey's moat, filled in by Charles II, was dug out in 1910 and its Tudor stone bridge rediscovered.

*Carved newel post in the Horn Room bearing the monogram of Queen Victoria.*

*Stained glass in the west window of the Great Hall, shows Henry VIII flanked by the arms of his six wives. The lower frames contain the arms of Henry's three surviving children, Edward VI, Mary I and Elizabeth I.*

## THE PALACE TODAY

TODAY Hampton Court Palace remains a royal palace and is used for state and other functions attended by members of the royal family. On display at the Palace are the paintings, furnishings and works of art in the State Apartments which form part of Her Majesty The Queen's Collection.

Hampton Court is very much a community, having among its residents distinguished servants of the crown occupying grace-and-favour apartments. The Chapel Royal has regular services and the Tudor Tennis Court has an associated club with a thriving membership. In recent years vacant apartments, particularly in the Tudor part of the Palace, have been allocated to craft organisations connected with historic buildings such as the Textile Conservation Centre, the Embroiderers Guild, the Royal School of Needlework and the Building Conservation Trust.

Both the Palace and gardens which are amongst the most important and beautiful in England, are open to the public year-round and attract many hundreds of thousands of visitors. Maintenance, restoration and improvement of both are an ongoing process carried out by a permanent work-force committed to the task of ensuring that one of the finest examples of our heritage will remain an important and enjoyable experience for both present and future generations of visitors.

*The 1986 fire gutted a private grace-and-favour attic floor apartment.*

23

# PLAN OF GROUND FLOOR APARTMENTS

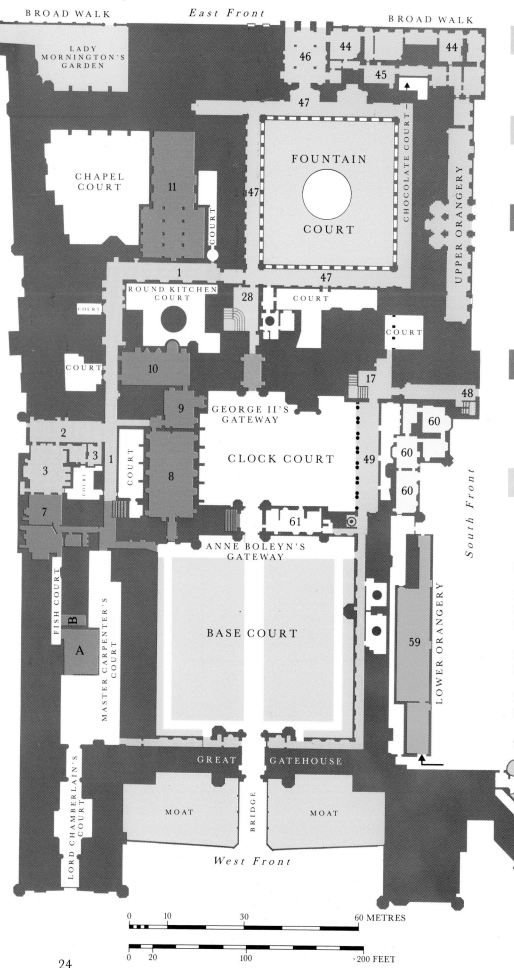

# PLAN OF FIRST FLOOR APARTMENTS

## Wren - First Floor

**Queen's Private Apartments**
36 Queen's Private Chapel
37 Queen's Bathing Closet
38 Private Dining Room
39 Closet
40 Queen's Private Chamber
41 King's Private Dressing Room
42 George II's Private Chamber

43 Law's Museum

## Wren - Ground Floor

44 **King's Private Apartments**

45 Law's Print Collection
46 Pillared Vestibule
47 Fountain Court Cloister
48 Beauty Staircase
49 Colonnade
50 Great Vine

## Eighteenth Century

51 Public Drawing Room
**Prince of Wales' Apartments**
52 Prince of Wales' Presence Chamber
53 Prince of Wales' Drawing Room
54 Prince of Wales' Bedchamber
55 Lobby
56 Prince of Wales' Staircase

57 Cumberland Suite

## Royal Collection

58 Renaissance Picture Gallery
59 Mantegna Gallery

## Hampton Court Palace

60 Exhibition
61 Gift Shop

 Grassed Areas

\*Rooms closed due to fire damage
(Re-opening Summer 1992)

● Ladies' Toilets

● Gentlemens' Toilets

◉ Disabled Toilet

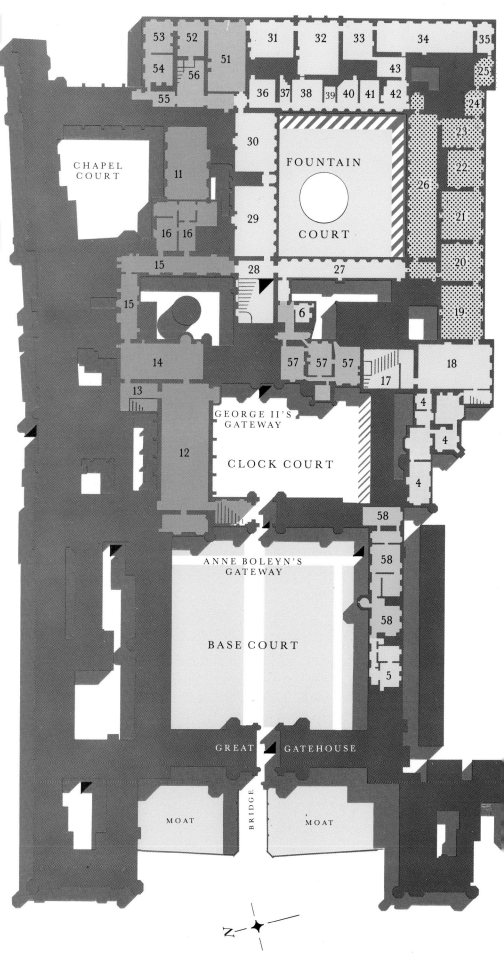

*Exterior*

The North Cloister, a
wide, dark passage, was
the main route for
servants carrying food
and drink from the
kitchens to the
Great Hall above.

## THE PALACE

*Hampton Court is not for the hurried visitor. A
treasure trove of royal history, architectural gems,
great paintings and stunning gardens, its delights
are best experienced at a leisurely pace, with
frequent rests along the way, simply to take stock.
Whether a student of history, a lover of beauty or
a keen gardener, there is something for everyone,
which is why many visitors come back time and
again. Hampton Court grows with the knowing.*

## COURTYARDS
## & CLOISTERS

THE MAIN PALACE entrance, close to the Thames
bridge, is through William III's Trophy gate. The
outer piers have lead trophies of arms and the inner
ones, the lion and unicorn. Supporting shields bear
the arms of George II. To the left of Outer Green
Court stand the former Palace barracks, now
converted to flats, offices and the Royal Mews
Exhibition.

*Trophy gate, around the turn of the century.
This rather plain gateway was built for William III
and altered for George II thirty years later.*

*Lead unicorn on the Trophy gate. One of a pair
originally cast in 1701 at a cost of £115, it was
repaired and embellished later in the century.*

The Dragon of Wales guards the entrance to the Palace. Although the King's Beasts date from this century, they replaced long-destroyed Tudor beasts which originally decorated the bridge.

## COURTYARDS & CLOISTERS

Ahead lies the west front of the Tudor palace built by Cardinal Wolsey and Henry VIII. Originally two storeys higher, the central gatehouse is entered over a bridge across the moat. On the parapets are the King's Beasts, the supporters of the royal arms. Above the gateway is a copy of the original panel carved with the arms of Henry VIII, who took over and enlarged Hampton Court after Wolsey's fall. Each turret has a terracotta roundel with the head of a Roman emperor, made for Wolsey by Giovanni da Maiano.

Despite the importance of the Thames to the south, the main entrance to the Palace has always been from the west, across the Outer Green Court and through Wolsey's Great Gatehouse.

Gargoyles in the form of fantastic monsters perch on the gable end of the Great Hall.

In 1742 the earliest guidebook to the Palace wondered why Wolsey had bought the Maiano roundel of Vitellius. He "had not one good quality to recommend him; but like the Cardinal was notorious for his dissolute and luxurious course of life."

# COURTYARDS & CLOISTERS

The first courtyard, Base Court, is much as Wolsey built it, and contained lodgings for his guests and large household. Over the entrance are Henry's arms and on the turrets flanking the arch are the badges and initials of Elizabeth I, his younger daughter. On the far side of Base Court stands the inner gatehouse, now named Anne Boleyn's Gateway, after Henry's second queen. The bell-turret above houses a bell that belonged to the Knights Hospitallers. Over the arch are Henry's arms, and on the turrets more terracotta medallions of Roman emperors.

Clock Court, the inner courtyard of Wolsey's house, has been much altered. To your left Henry's Great Hall rises sheer, with its lofty buttresses topped with gilded vanes. Over the gateway in Wolsey's west range are his arms supported by *putti* (cherubs) and surmounted by his cardinal's hat, all in terracotta, an early example of the then new Renaissance style. Below them is his motto, *Dominus michi adjutor* – The Lord is my helper. Higher up is the famous Astronomical Clock made for Henry in 1540 by Nicholas Oursian, Deviser of the King's Horologies. It shows the hour, month, day, number of days since the beginning of the year, and phases of the moon. The sun revolves around the earth as the clock was contrived before the discoveries of Galileo and Copernicus.

*Base Court was always the 'business' area of the Palace, Wolsey's household was lodged here and the quadrangle later provided accommodation for government officials and politicians attending the monarch.*

*Wolsey's arms on Anne Boleyn's gateway were obliterated when Henry VIII took over the Palace. His mottos, monogram and arms were covered by those of the King in lead or stone cladding and his cardinal's hat disappeared beneath a wrought iron crown. They were discovered and restored in 1845.*

*The astronomical clock has been repeatedly repaired and its mechanism renewed. Dials indicate the phases of the moon and time of high water at London Bridge, vital information in the days when tides governed travel to and from the Palace.*

*A royal beast surveys the scene from the highest point of the Palace — the roof of the Great Hall.*

*Fountain Court takes its name from the central fountain added in 1702.*

*Window surrounds carved by William Emmett in 1691-2 at a rate of £20 per window. The decorations of foliage and lion skins are an allusion to Hercules, a favourite hero of William III.*

*When the gateway on the east side of Base Court was rebuilt in the 1730s, the Prime Minister, Sir Robert Walpole, insisted that the new work should be designed to match Wolsey's Tudor brickwork around it.*

The date 1732 above George II's Gateway ahead, marks William Kent's remodelling of the east range of Clock Court. This example of eighteenth century Gothic is the earliest attempt at Hampton Court to match the original Tudor style. Fountain Court was designed by Sir Christopher Wren for William III, to replace Henry's Cloister Green Court. From its east cloister walk, a semicircular bay opens into a pillared vestibule leading out into the gardens on the east front.

Above the arched cloisters of Fountain Court are the tall windows of the State Apartments. The square windows at attic level lit lodgings provided for the court. On the west side a first floor gallery, topped by a balustrade, screens the Tudor buildings behind. Carved wreaths in the form of lion-skins surround the circular windows. On the south side, which is currently being restored following the fire, the wreaths frame twelve panels which depicted *The Labours of Hercules,* painted by Louis Laguerre.

*The Wolsey Rooms have been altered and restored, but many features have survived. The plain Tudor fireplaces and linenfold panelling date from the first half of the sixteenth century.*

# WOLSEY ROOMS & CLOSET

T HE WOLSEY ROOMS are thought to have been the Cardinal's private apartments. The first two rooms feature Tudor linenfold panelling. The central room has later panelling and a ribbed ceiling with early Renaissance decorative motifs. The ceiling of the end room features Wolsey's badges. Two rooms are hung with north Italian seventeenth century needlework panels. A doorway opens into the Beauty Staircase which leads to William III's former Private Dining Room, where Sir Godfrey Kneller's portraits known as the Hampton Court Beauties formerly hung.

Through the window of the Wolsey Closet visitors can see where Wren's building was superimposed on to the Tudor palace. Visitors get a delightful glimpse of the decoration and colour of the lost Tudor interiors. Sixteenth century panels show scenes from Christ's Passion. The ceiling is a chequerwork of badges and ornaments with Tudor roses, Prince of Wales's feathers, and Renaissance motifs. Tudor badges, mermaids, dolphins and vases decorate the frieze. Wolsey's motto is repeated below.

*The Wolsey Closet provides our only glimpse of the colour and richness which marked the interior of Wolsey's palace. The pictures of the Last Supper and Scourging are Tudor but are painted over work of the previous century. The panels came from an earlier building.*

*Gilded Renaissance motifs and richly coloured badges decorate the ceiling of the Wolsey Closet.*

*Tudor*

*The hammer-beam roof of the Great Hall. The richly decorated pendants were carved by Richard Rydge of London, and show the growing influence of the Italian Renaissance.*

*Elizabethan visitors to Hampton Court were told that the roof of the Great Hall had been made out of special Irish timber which "will bear nothing poisonous, consequently not even spiders", and which "has the natural property of keeping free of cobwebs". In reality, no Irish wood seems to have been used and most of the timber came from less enchanted forests in the Home Counties.*

## TUDOR PALACE

T HE GREAT HALL has a huge hammer-beam roof, enriched with carving and tracery. Amidst the carved foliage of the main supports are Henry's arms, in places impaling those of Anne Boleyn. Her badges and initials also decorate the roof but some have been replaced by those of Jane Seymour. A fan-vaulted bay window lights the dais, on which stood the high table for senior members of the household. The rest of the company sat at tables in the Hall itself. Smoke from an open hearth in the middle of the Hall escaped through a roof louvre, long removed. The Flemish tapestries which show the story of Abraham, belonged to Henry VIII. The Hall continues to be used for prestigious banquets, often with musical accompaniment from the Minstrel's Gallery which is above the oak screen at the low end of the Hall.

*Painted head and elaborate tracery from the Great Hall roof.*

# TUDOR PALACE

The Great Watching Chamber was the outer chamber of Henry's vanished state apartments. Its restored ceiling comprises intersecting ribs which curve down to form pendants. Roundels in the spaces between depict the arms and badges of Henry and Jane Seymour, his third queen. The stained glass of the bay window, by Thomas Willement in 1841, depicts the arms and badges of Henry and Wolsey. The Flemish tapestries may have been Wolsey's.

The Haunted Gallery is said to be visited by the ghost of Catherine Howard, Henry VIII's fifth wife. The Gallery was built by Wolsey to link the Chapel with his State Apartments. Its windows look out on to Round Kitchen Court. The Flemish tapestries may have belonged to Elizabeth I.

The Royal Pew of the Chapel Royal is where members of the royal family traditionally worshipped. From here can be seen the main part of the Chapel with its timber vaulted ceiling. Its carved and gilded pendants date from 1535-36. The rest of the decoration, including Thornhill's painting and Gibbons's oak reredos, dates from Wren's refitting for Queen Anne. The windows, altered by Wren, were replaced in original form in 1894. The *trompe l'oeil* window on the far right, painted by Thornhill, preserves the form of Wren's windows. The Chapel is open for public worship on Sundays and other feast days.

*Several ghosts supposedly stalk the Palace, including Queens Jane Seymour and Catherine Howard.*

*Great Watching Chamber. Originally a guard room, it served the Tudor royal apartments.*

*Visitors in the sixteenth century were struck by the richness of the Chapel, and particularly by the Queen's "closet", which was "quite transparent, having its window of chrystal".*

## TUDOR KITCHENS
### *Ground Floor*

North Cloister was the main route for servants carrying food and drink to the Great Hall and royal apartments above. Stout oak posts support the floor of the Great Hall above the Beer Cellar. The eastern section of the Tudor Great Kitchens was almost certainly built for Wolsey. Inside the large fireplace in the north wall, a smaller one and brick ovens were later inserted. Food intended for the Horn Room would have been passed through the oak-framed hatches.

The Kitchen which was added for Henry was partitioned in the seventeenth century. It has three great open fireplaces, and two stone hatches opening into a second serving place, from which food for diners in the main body of the hall was carried.

Fish Court was one of the small service courts around which subsidiary kitchens and offices, with lodgings above, were grouped. Through its door, raw food, or food prepared or partly prepared elsewhere, must have entered the Great Kitchens. Around other small courts were situated a pastry and confectionery, saucery, spicery, boiling-house, acatry (supplying meat and fish), larders and sculleries. The kitchens fell out of use after George III abandoned the Palace.

*Fish Court. One of a series of ancillary courts on the north side of the Palace. Around them were grouped the warren of cellars, specialist kitchens and offices which served the main kitchen.*

*Great Kitchen. Begun by Wolsey but greatly extended by Henry VIII, it is one of the largest and best preserved Tudor kitchens in the country.*

*King's Wine and Beer Cellars. Situated beneath the Great Hall and Watching Chamber they stored the huge quantity of alcohol required by the Tudor court. Even servants received a daily allowance of beer and wine — a gallon or more per person — which appears generous, if not lethal, to modern eyes. In those days it was often unwise to drink untreated water or milk, and watery beer or wine — much weaker than modern brews — provided almost the only safe and plentiful drink.*

*Wren*

*William III and Mary II – Britain's first joint monarchs.*

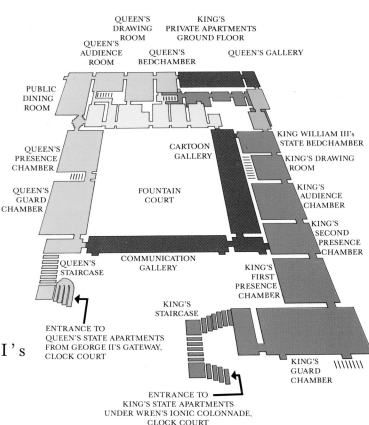

QUEEN'S DRAWING ROOM

KING'S PRIVATE APARTMENTS GROUND FLOOR

QUEEN'S AUDIENCE ROOM

QUEEN'S BEDCHAMBER

QUEEN'S GALLERY

PUBLIC DINING ROOM

QUEEN'S PRESENCE CHAMBER

CARTOON GALLERY

KING WILLIAM III's STATE BEDCHAMBER

KING'S DRAWING ROOM

QUEEN'S GUARD CHAMBER

FOUNTAIN COURT

KING'S AUDIENCE CHAMBER

KING'S SECOND PRESENCE CHAMBER

QUEEN'S STAIRCASE

COMMUNICATION GALLERY

KING'S FIRST PRESENCE CHAMBER

KING'S STAIRCASE

KING'S GUARD CHAMBER

ENTRANCE TO QUEEN'S STATE APARTMENTS FROM GEORGE II'S GATEWAY, CLOCK COURT

ENTRANCE TO KING'S STATE APARTMENTS UNDER WREN'S IONIC COLONNADE, CLOCK COURT

# WILLIAM III & MARY II's STATE & PRIVATE APARTMENTS

THE STATE and Private Apartments occupy the ground and first floors of Wren's building. Each suite is approached by a grand staircase, leading to a guard chamber, presence chamber, audience (or privy) chamber, drawing room and state bedchamber. The name of each room is above the door leading into the next room. Behind the State Apartments, back stairs communicate with the other floors, where the court and royal household lodged.

It is important to understand that Wren's Palace is an extension of the Tudor Palace which you see from the main gate. Built for William III and Mary II in 1689, the King and Queen were to have separate state and private apartments, set on two floors around Fountain Court.

*North wall of the King's Staircase, painted in 1701-2, showing Ceres holding a sheaf of corn and pointing to loaves of bread, surrounded by nymphs, cupids and other gods. It was probably designed to portray the peace and plenty which William III had brought.*

*The arrangement of royal accommodation was determined by tradition. The King and Queen each had a suite of rooms comprising both state apartments — grand chambers for receiving visitors, conducting business and hosting official functions — and a set of private apartments. The King's and Queen's state rooms were on the first floor and both were approached from the west via a grand staircase and a guard chamber. Moving from west to east, the rooms became progressively less "public" and admission to them more selective. Only a few trusted companions would have had access to the private apartments on the ground and first floor on the eastern side of the court.*

# KING'S STATE APARTMENTS

The King's Staircase has a fine wrought-iron balustrade by Jean Tijou. The decoration is by Antonio Verrio; its subject an obscure complex political allegory. The walls of the King's Guard Chamber are lined with more than 3000 arms, in a pattern designed by William III's gunsmith, Harris.

■ KING'S STATE APARTMENTS

☐ QUEEN'S STATE APARTMENTS

▨ KING'S PRIVATE APARTMENTS

☐ QUEEN'S PRIVATE APARTMENTS

\\\\\ PRIVATE STAIRCASES

*Walls and ceiling of the King's Staircase painted by Verrio, whose signature appears by the door into the Guard Chamber. Like many early visitors to the Palace, Horace Walpole was critical of the work and wrote that Verrio had painted the staircase "as ill as if he had spoiled it out of principle".*

*The King's Guard Chamber, by James Stephanoff, from W H Pyne's* History of the Royal Residences, *1819.*

*The arms in the King's Guard Chamber are still arranged in the decorative pattern laid out around 1700. The designer William III's gunsmith, Harris, was rewarded with a royal pension. In the eighteenth century every piece was removed, cleaned and replaced each spring.*

# QUEEN'S STATE APARTMENTS

As Mary II died before Hampton Court was completed her Apartments were fitted out and furnished during later reigns.

The Queen's Staircase has a wrought-iron balustrade by Tijou. The walls and ceilings were painted by Kent in 1734. A great allegorical painting by Honthorst shows Charles I and his queen as Jupiter and Juno receiving the seven Liberal Arts who are presented to the Duke of Buckingham in the guise of Mercury.

Kneller's *Hampton Court Beauties* line the walls of the Queen's Guard Chamber. The monumental chimneypiece is by Sir John Vanbrugh and much of the carving is by Grinling Gibbons. This room is often used for receptions attended by the royal family.

The Queen's Presence Chamber contains Queen Anne's Bed. The boldly modelled ceiling was designed by Sir John Vanbrugh as was the chimney-piece, and together with the interior of the Queen's Guard Chamber, dates from the reign of George I.

*Marble chimneypiece in the Queen's Guard Chamber, one of a series of rooms decorated by Vanbrugh in 1716-18 for the Prince and Princess of Wales. It is typical of the bold style of these rooms, featuring lifesize Yeoman of the Guard.*

*Queen's Staircase. Built in the 1690s, the walls and ceilings were not painted until 1734. The Victorian historian, Ernest Law, was very scathing of Kent's work and accorded him "the doubtful honour of having besmeared the ceiling and walls of this staircase with paint".*

*Queen's Presence Chamber. Decorated by Vanbrugh in 1716-18 it has a large chimneypiece and an unpainted ceiling. The bed and furniture were made for Queen Anne's apartments at Windsor in 1714, and are part of the Royal Collection.*

*The Nine Muses, Jacopo Tintoretto. Royal Collection, Hampton Court Palace. This large painting was acquired by Charles I as part of the Mantua Collection. It was sold for £100 in 1651.*

The Queen's Audience Chamber, fitted out in George I's reign for George and Caroline, the Prince and Princess of Wales, includes a tapestry depicting Abraham. The room also contains the original Canopy of State. The Public Dining Room is so named because George II sometimes dined here in public. Planned as a Music or Dancing Room, its decoration was supervised by Vanbrugh.

*Care was taken to align Fountain Court with the existing eastern park, so that the centre window of the east front — in the Queen's Drawing Room — looks directly along the central avenue of the Fountain Garden and the Long Water.*

*Verrio's paintings in the Queen's Drawing Room glorify Queen Anne. On the ceiling she is Justice, attended by Neptune, Britannia, Peace and Plenty; on the west wall she receives honours and tributes from the four quarters of the globe.*

*Paintings on the walls in the Queen's Drawing Room celebrate British naval power under Anne's husband, Prince George, the Lord Admiral. On the north wall he is shown in splendid attire before the fleet. He appears again on the south wall, nude, portly and riding a miserable looking dolphin.*

The Queen's Drawing Room temporarily contains King William's bed, rescued from the fire damaged area. Verrio's decorations celebrate British naval power in the reign of Anne, successor to William. The middle window of the room commands a fine view of the gardens, one of the best surviving examples of Baroque planning in England. Three avenues radiate in a *patte d'oie* — goose-foot pattern – to intersect a double semicircle of trees and water extending across Home Park. The middle avenue encloses the Long Water, and dates from Charles II's reign.

The ceiling of the Queen's Bedroom, painted by James Thornhill for George I, depicts Apollo about to enter his chariot. On its deep cove are medallion portraits of George I, George II and Queen Caroline, as Prince and Princess of Wales, and their son Frederick, later Prince of Wales and the father of George III. The state bed, chairs and stools were made in 1715 for George and Caroline but only the bed retains its original crimson damask upholstery.

*Tulip vases were made for William III and Mary II during the 1690s especially for Hampton Court and are part of the Royal Collection. Bulbs were planted within each tier and the growing shoots would then naturally emerge through the open spouts and bloom. The most elaborate examples have up to eleven tiers and stack in the form of a pagoda. Each section was made to fit exactly into the next, so that a tier from one vase usually does not fit into the corresponding space in*

*The Queen's Gallery, by Richard Cattermole, from W H Pyne's History of the Royal Residences, 1818. When the court was in residence, entertainments were often held here and the gallery was sometimes known as the Ball Room.*

*Spectacular marble chimneypiece by John Nost. Originally intended for the King's Bedchamber, it was moved to the Queen's Gallery in 1701.*

The Queen's Gallery has a cornice by Gibbons and a marble chimneypiece by John Nost. The Brussels tapestries, of 1662, tell the story of Alexander the Great. The blue and white Delft china vases, made for William and Mary, bear their arms and cipher, and the motto of the House of Orange.

Queen Mary's Closet at the end of the Queen's Gallery is closed to the public as it leads into the fire-damaged area. It was originally hung with needlework done by Mary II and her ladies.

The Queen's Private Apartments were originally designed by Wren for Mary II. A series of smaller intimate rooms, the doors in the rear walls lead into the grand State Apartments behind, which overlook the gardens. Part of Mary's collection of blue and white china is on display throughout the suite. The Queen's Private Chapel or Oratory was decorated for Queen Caroline, wife of George II. Her chaplain prayed while she dressed in the adjacent Closet, with its marble basin.

*The King's Private Dressing Room (above) and the Private Dining Room (at right). From 1795 to 1802, these and the adjoining small rooms were occupied by the Stadtholder of the Netherlands, who had fled from his own country in the face of a French invasion.*

*Flemish Fair, by Jan Breughel.*
*Royal Collection, Hampton Court Palace.*

The Private Dining Room includes paintings by Pellegrini. A second Closet with a water closet opening off, leads to the Queen's Private Chamber, where there is another basin. The King's Private Dressing Room has Gibbons carvings on the chimneybreast and an eighteenth century travelling bed hung with crimson damask. In George II's Private Chamber the flock wallpaper is early nineteenth century. The pattern is still produced.

*The walls of George II's Private Chamber are decorated with coloured flock paper, dating from the early nineteenth century.*

Law's Museum is named after Ernest Law, a Victorian grace-and-favour resident who wrote a three-volume history of Hampton Court and pressed for the restoration of the Tudor buildings.

# KING'S PRIVATE APARTMENTS
*Ground Floor*

On display in the King's Private Apartments are pictures from the Royal Collection. Three closets are partly furnished to suggest their appearance in William's time. A passageway looks out on to a small internal court called Chocolate Court, which derives its name from William's passion for chocolate. Beyond this, another room contains prints and engravings of the palace and gardens from Ernest Law's collection.

*Part of a surround in one of the closets in the Private Apartments, featuring birds, flowers and musical instruments. In 1699 "Grinling Gibbons, carver" was paid just over £5 for "23 ft of looking glass frame" in these apartments.*

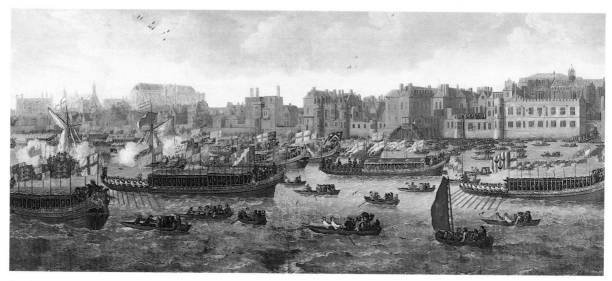

*Lord Mayor's Water Procession, artist unknown. Royal Collection, Hampton Court Palace. Charles II can be seen on the balcony of Whitehall Palace, in the background. The painting, which is thought to represent the procession of Sir Henry Tulse in 1683, provides one of the most detailed views of the river front of Whitehall Palace, before its alteration and destruction under William III.*

*William III's writing desk may be the "escritoire of walnutt-tree" ordered for the Private Apartments in 1700. These rooms were always well furnished by the monarch. Royal Collection, Hampton Court Palace.*

## Eighteenth Century

*Judith with the Head of Holofernes, by Allesandro Allori. Royal Collection, Hampton Court Palace. Tradition has it that Allori modelled Judith upon his mistress, with whom he had fallen out, and that he painted himself as Holofernes.*

*During George II's visits to the Palace in the 1730s, much of Kent's new east range of Clock Court accommodated the King's second son, William Augustus, Duke of Cumberland, and his small retinue of servants and tutors.*

*Prince of Wales' Presence Chamber. Part of the suite fitted up in 1716-18 for Prince George, later George II. At one time, a canopy and chair of state would have stood in this room.*

## CUMBERLAND SUITE

THE CUMBERLAND SUITE which Kent designed in 1732 for William, Duke of Cumberland, comprises two reception rooms, a bedchamber and a closet. The plaster ceilings, marble chimneypieces and bed alcove are typical of Kent's work.

## PRINCE OF WALES' APARTMENTS

THE PRINCE OF WALES' Suite, largely by Vanbrugh, was also used by George and Caroline and later by their son Frederick, Prince of Wales. Beyond the Presence Chamber, the Drawing Room is decorated to show how it was furnished for Frederick in 1731.

From the window visitors get an unexpected glimpse of Lady Mornington's Garden, the private refuge of the Duke of Wellington's mother when she was a grace-and-favour resident. Also visible is the Tudor brickwork of Henry VIII's Close Tennis Court, converted in the 1670s to accommodate James II and his wife when Duke and Duchess of York.

# PRINCE OF WALES' APARTMENTS

The Prince of Wales' Bedchamber contains a bed designed for Charlotte, George III's queen and recently restored by the Tapestry Conservation Studio at Hampton Court. In the Lobby leading to the Prince of Wales' Staircase is Leonard Knyff's famous bird's-eye view of Hampton Court, painted about 1700. It shows the elaborate formal gardens laid out for William III.

The balcony outside the door of the Presence Chamber has elaborate wrought-iron festoons below the landing. Tapestries on the walls of the staircase, woven at Mortlake, depict The Battle of Solebay at Southwold in Suffolk in 1672 between the English and Dutch fleets.

*Queen Charlotte and her husband, George III, are usually associated with the removal of furniture from the Palace. But her richly decorated bed, with its elaborate tester, which has travelled the other way is in the Prince of Wales' Bedchamber. Part of the Royal Collection, it was made in the 1770s and perhaps intended for Windsor.*

*Charles I, Henrietta Maria and Jeffrey Hudson, by Daniel Mytens.*
*Royal Collection, Hampton Court Palace.*
*Hudson, a dwarf, was presented to the Queen in a pie and entered her service. He fled into exile after killing a man in a duel. His opponent had treated the challenge as a joke and came armed only with a water pistol. The King and Queen are seen in hunting costume.*

*Five of the six tapestries depicting the Battle of Solebay are now at Hampton Court. Part of the Royal Collection, they were woven by the Poyntz family at Mortlake and Hatton Garden during the 1680s and are made of silk and wool.*

*Weaver's mark, Solebay tapestry.*

*Royal
Collection*

*The Holy Family
with St Jerome
by Antonio Corregio.
Royal Collection,
Renaissance Gallery,
Hampton Court Palace.*

## RENAISSANCE GALLERY

SOME of the most important pictures in the Palace are on show in the Renaissance Gallery. Part of the Royal Collection, the display includes pictures from the sixteenth and seventeenth century by German and Flemish painters such as Cranach, Joos van Cleve, Provoost, Steenwyck and Neefs. The Italian paintings include masterpieces by Corregio, Dosso, Dossi, Lotto, Franciabigio, Parmigianino and Titian. The selection of pictures on display is changed from time to time.

## MANTEGNA GALLERY

*The Vase Bearer, No. IV,
part of the Triumphs of Caesar cartoon,
by Andrea Mantegna.
Royal Collection, Hampton Court Palace.*

The Lower Orangery houses one of the greatest works in the Royal Collection. It is also one of the supreme works of the Italian Renaissance. Nine canvasses make up the *Triumph(s) of Julius Caesar* by Andrea Mantegna. Painted at the court of the Gonzagas in Mantua *circa* 1492, the paintings were acquired by Charles I in 1629. Restored in 1969, the canvasses combine to create one of the grandest evocations of classical antiquity. They present an unrivalled synthesis between archeological exactitude and poetic imagination.

*Major restoration of the Mantegna cartoons was completed in 1969.
Only one of them, No. VII,* The Prisoners, *could not be freed of extensive
overpainting, which probably dates from the time of William III.*

The east front pillared vestibule opens onto the Broad Walk through wrought-iron screens by Jean Tijou. Laid out in 1700, the Broad Walk extends over a distance of nearly half a mile.

## THE PALACE GARDENS

WREN designed his new building to fit the existing garden layout with its formal canal and flanking avenue designed for Charles II. Hampton Court was his largest secular commission, integrating buildings and gardens into a vast formal landscape. Seen from the gardens, the regular classical facade of Wren's east front contrasts strikingly with the picturesque Tudor turrets, gables and chimneys to the north. In meeting William's wish to reduce the number of steps, Wren kept the level of the first floor low. The size of the windows reflects the relative importance of the rooms.

*South front of the newly completed Fountain Court, dated circa 1700. In the foreground is Fanelli's Diana Fountain, which had been moved to Hampton Court from Somerset House at the command of Oliver Cromwell. The fountain was removed in 1701 and re-erected in 1713 on a new base at its present site in Bushy Park.*

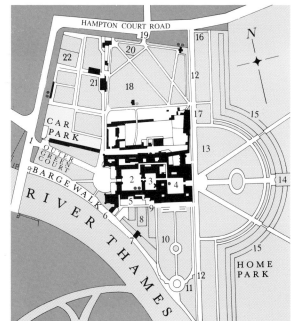

The great stone centrepiece, focal point of the whole design, is surmounted by a giant pediment containing Caius Gabriel Cibber's relief of Hercules triumphing over Envy. Corinthian columns support the pediment and flank the three windows of the Queen's Drawing Room. The windows are extra long, their sills resting directly over the opening to the ground floor vestibule which has decorative wrought-iron screens by Jean Tijou. Over the middle window is a symbolic composition of trumpets, sceptre and crown, incorporating William and Mary's cipher.

*Hampton Court Palace from the south, showing the Tijou screen, Privy Garden and the south front of Fountain Court as it appeared before the fire of 1986.*

## PLAN OF THE PALACE & GARDENS

| | |
|---|---|
| 1 Trophy Gate | 14 Long Water |
| 2 Base Court | 15 Canal |
| 3 Clock Court | 16 Flowerpot Gates |
| 4 Fountain Court | 17 Royal Tennis Court |
| 5 Lower Orangery | 18 Wilderness |
| Mantegna Gallery | 19 Lion Gates |
| 6 Great Vine | 20 The Maze |
| 7 Banqueting House | 21 Restaurant & Cafeteria |
| 8 Pond Garden | 22 Tiltyard Gardens |
| 9 Knot Garden | ● Ladies' Toilets |
| 10 Privy Garden | ● Gentlemen's Toilets |
| 11 Tijou Screen | |
| 12 Broad Walk | |
| 13 Fountain Garden | |

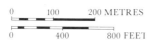

0    100    200 METRES
0    400    800 FEET

*The great centrepiece of the East Front. Immediately above the grand windows of the drawing room are carvings of vases with fruit and flowers and a centre panel featuring the royal crown, horns and the monogram of William III and Mary II.*

*East Front during the reign of George II.*
*Conical clipped yews are a prominent feature.*

The east front vestibule opens on to the Broad Walk, a wide gravel terrace extending from the Flower Pot Gate on the Kingston Road to the River Thames. During Queen Anne's reign, wide lawns with clipped yews and hollies replaced William's Dutch parterre with its trimmed box hedges, fountains and statues. Queen Anne is said to have disliked the smell of box. At the south end of the east front visitors may pass from the Broad Walk through a gateway with handsome stone piers to a terrace facing the south front and down shallow steps to the Privy Garden. Along the east side a raised terrace overlooks the Garden and the Broad Walk.

On the opposite side is Queen Mary's Bower – an alley of hornbeam. The far end of the garden is bounded by the Thames-side Barge Walk. Its name recalls the working barges which were once towed along from the river bank. The famous Tijou Screen, twelve superb wrought-iron gates or panels, now stands here.

Major restoration work resulting from the fire is now in progress along the south front. Over the centre window a trophy of arms with the Latin inscription GULIELMUS ET MARIA R (EX) R (EGINA) F (ECERUNT) records the building of the new palace by William and Mary.

*Jean Tijou supplied most of the ornamental ironwork at the Palace during the reigns of William III and Queen Anne including ornamental weather vanes, balustrades and the famous garden screens.*

*William III's Banqueting House is located behind one of the Pond Gardens. These intricate gardens have been restored in formal Stuart style.*

At the west end of the south front terrace, a gateway opens on to a walk flanked on the left by small formal gardens within Tudor brick walls. In the angle between Wren's addition and the Tudor buildings lies the Knot Garden planted in 1924 to show the type of garden fashionable in Elizabeth I's time. To the left of Wren's south front are the windows of the Wolsey Rooms. A restored lead cupola caps the angle turret.

The detached Banqueting House overlooking the river may have been designed by William Talman, Comptroller of the King's Works and Deputy Superintendent of the Gardens under William III. Verrio decorated its Great (or Painted) Room. It is one of Hampton Court's most important Baroque interiors.

Partly hiding the back of the south range of Base Court is the Lower Orangery, now a gallery exhibiting Mantegna's paintings of the *Triumph of Caesar*. The adjacent Vinery houses the Great Vine, planted in 1768, and it still produces a large crop of Black Hamburg grapes.

*In the nineteenth century the Banqueting House was used as a private grace-and-favour residence. In 1864 the new tenant, Miss Baly, was shocked by "the large undressed figures on each side of the fireplace" and wanted them "either draped or clouded in such manner as to render them appropriate decorations".*

*The Music Party: Frederick, Prince of Wales, with his three eldest sisters, by Philip Mercier. Royal Collection. Set in the Banqueting House, Hampton Court Palace can be seen through the window in the background. Painted around 1733, when Prince Frederick began learning the cello, Lord Hervey reported that by 1734 it was his practice when at Kensington to "sing French and Italian songs to his own playing, for an hour or two together, while his audience was composed of all the under servants and rabble of the Palace".*

*The Great Vine was attracting attention as early as 1800 and during the nineteenth century could produce over 2000 lbs of grapes in a good year. The roots may have found an old palace cesspit or a band of rich river silt.*

# THE PALACE GARDENS

North of Wren's building is the converted Tudor Close Tennis Court, partly hidden by a wall. Along the Broad Walk a door leads into the Royal Tennis Court, built in the 1620s. Visitors may be fortunate enough to see a game in progress. Beyond the Tennis Court, a large gateway in the wall opens from the Broad Walk into the Wilderness. Only a few paths and the famous Maze, a labyrinth of hedges, survive of the late seventeenth century layout. The Maze is open to the public. A diagonal path leads to the Lion Gate, which Wren intended as the Palace's new grand entrance. Its stonework bears Anne's monogram. The ironwork dates from the reign of George I.

Directly opposite, in Bushy Park, begins the mile-long Chestnut Avenue, with its inner rows of chestnuts, flanked on each side by four rows of limes. The Diana Fountain stands in the centre of the Great Basin, which the Avenue divides to enclose. West of the Wilderness extend lawns, flower beds and a rose garden on the site of the Tiltyard where Henry watched tournaments. One of its viewing towers can still be seen.

*The early Stuart Tennis Court is still in perfect order and hosts the British Open Real Tennis Championships. Pepys watched Charles II play here, though he was sickened "to see how the King's play was extolled without any cause at all".*

*Quando pila et Sphæræ flectuntur corporis artus,*
*Corpus erit levius, pectus erit levius.*

*So oft ich thue den Ballen schlagn,*
*Erfrisch ich mir Hertz tragen vnd magn.*

*Sixteenth century German engraving of a game of tennis.*

*One of Jerome K Jerome's* Three Men in a Boat *declared the maze "very simple . . . it's absurd to call it a maze", only to become completely lost. Inside he met other visitors "who had given up all hopes of ever seeing their home and friends again".*